Where is the Ladybug?

Copyright © 2021 Diana Damoc
All rights reserved.

Where is the Ladybug?

Learn about

In, On, Under

DIANA DAMOC

Where is the Ladybug?

The Ladybug is on the flower.

Where is the Ladybug?

The Ladybug is **in** the tree.

Where is the Ladybug?

The Ladybug is in the grass.

Where is the Ladybug?

The Ladybug is under the dog.

Where is the Ladybug?

The Ladybug is under the car.

Where is the Ladybug?

The Ladybug is on the bike.

Where is the Ladybug?

The Ladybug is in the nest.

Where is the Ladybug?

The Ladybug is on the branch.

Where is the Ladybug?

The Ladybug is **under** the shelf.

Where is the Ladybug?

The Ladybug is under the armchair.

Where is the Ladybug?

The Ladybug is under the couch.

Where is the Ladybug?

The Ladybug is under the lamp.

Where is the Ladybug?

The Ladybug is in the box.

Where is the Ladybug?

The Ladybug is in the bowl.

Where is the Ladybug?

The Ladybug is on the lemon.

Where is the Ladybug?

The Ladybug is on the pineapple.

Where is the Ladybug?

The Ladybug is on the strawberry.

Where is the Ladybug?

The Ladybug is on the shoe.

Printed in Great Britain
by Amazon